NEXT AGE
BUSINESS

TABLE OF CONTENTS

DEDICATION

I Dedicate this book to all Strappers, that were, are, and will be.

A Big thank you to all those who showed me the path of innovation and technology development. All the mentors who took time to sit down with me over lunch, coffee, or over the phone.

Thank you all.

May our accomplishments be worthy of our ambitions,

This is for the future.

PREFACE

As time evolves and humanity with it, it seems more and more obvious that there may be some cycle in the evolution of Mankind. Not only has this idea of cycles been a belief anchored in many civilizations from China to the Mayas and all religions in between, but also in modern times, we have been taught, for example, that the economy goes through cycles (recession every 7 to 8 years). That concept of cycles has also found its way into the world of technology. The most famous example may be Moore's Law, which is the observation that, over the history of computing hardware, the number of transistors in a dense integrated circuit has doubled approximately every two years.

In today's hyperactive technology startup scene, there is a lot that can be said regarding the cycle of life of a startup, or the cycles known as "growth stages" in the startup world, or again the cycles of dilution which often go hand in hand with the cycles known as "rounds of funding".

The main point here is that no matter how we look at it, from the largest macro level to the smallest micro level, it truly seems that everything is following some kind of cycle, and maybe the naturalists, the old shamans, and all the traditional belief systems like Ayurveda (who believe and live by "cycles"), are right.

One can easily see how seasons change and even us as Humans (both men and women) follow certain cycles. Some on a yearly basis, some on a monthly basis, and also some on a daily basis.

In this essay, we shall try to navigate through some of the current technological shifts (reflecting further on The Manifesto of The Digital Revolution), however, the core focus will be on how the standard entrepreneurship cycles Startups usually tend to go through cycles. We will also attempt to identify what we think are some limits to the current models of entrepreneurship in technology startups, an attempt will be made to show an innovative model of business entrepreneurship which should, when applied, offer a new model for the future: Next Age Business.

Jay - Strapdoor, Inc. –

Fall 2016- Remain Innocent – Make New Ways

Note from the Author: This document is sparse in structure; however, this is on purpose. It has been put together over a few months by consolidating ideation and data. While I was going to make it a multiple chapter book, afterl thought, the most important part will be to get the info out there. So the record will be made for those who may be searching, or may need to know. Included in the end is the complete tools we used to implement our model. May it guide entrepreneurial growth

Chapter 1: Recap of the Manifesto

A snapshot of 2015 in tech developments and prediction on the future of the Web

As at the beginning of the year 2016, it seemed that the industry trends identified in the Manifesto a year prior are on target. Internet of Things, Cloud Computing, and Big data, remain some of the hottest areas of development and investment in the Tech scene. 2 areas we did not touch on were Virtual Reality and Fin Tech.

V.R / A.R

It seems clear that the time of the long lasting dream of Virtual Reality has arrived. Although this idea has been around since the 80's (there used to be a huge experiment center in Sunnyvale, CA which was abandoned due to epilepsy risks), it seems it is only now that the technology has gotten good enough to become an actual consumer product which can be used by lots of people. Not only have the hardware and software advancements allowed this, but one could argue that the ubiquitous cell phone devices in everyone's pockets are also a key factor in user adoption. Indeed, it was surprising to find out that V.R is actually displayed on the phone screen. One could easily think (like I did) that the V.R experience is a stand-alone experience, while in fact, all what the headset does is that it magnifies the split images which are displayed on the cellular phone device! A little disappointing, although I have to admit some of the experiences are pretty cool and do give a sense of immersion like nothing before it. There are some all integrated solutions, but none mobile yet. The real fun will begin when full quality and interaction has been figured out for mobile and eventually when price goes down.

Let's look at some strengths and weaknesses of VR

Strengths	Weaknesses
Entertaining	Needs improvements in graphics fps
Good quality graphics	Acknowledged risks on brain / vision
Interesting applications	Used for a limited time
Super community	Limited content
Cool interactive scenarios	No awareness of surroundings.

The next layer above and beyond Virtual Reality is Augmented Reality. In augmented reality, the "headset" allows you to see your surrounding and somehow projects information and visuals in your field of view. The technology has a lot more work to be done on it before it can become an actual mass consumer product. I was able to see some interesting industrial applications such as the AR construction helmet which will display different information on the construction worker surroundings (such as wear and tear of parts, temperatures of pipes, and allow for instant ordering of needed parts). Another great example was the welding training station using Augmented Reality which offers a safe and effective way to train welders, without any material cost and excellent precision. However, the technology is still far from becoming a major consumer product and will need a lot more research and development before it makes its way to the mainstream user.

FIN-TECH

If you haven't heard the term before: "Financial technology, also known as **FinTech**, is a line of business based on using software to provide financial services. Financial technology companies are generally startups founded with the purpose of disrupting incumbent financial systems and corporations that rely less on software". (Wikipedia)

Needless to explain why this has become a huge sector; with London as its capital, big financial institutions have been massively funding the startups, leading to a big influx of entrepreneurs in the field trying to come up with the next software solution to financial issues. From payment processing to peer to peer money transfers, the industry is booming and will probably remain dynamic for a few years until the dust settles and we come up with the new financial systems and banking methods of the next century.

Although a lot of software systems have been developed early on for financial institutions, the innovation has now moved to the startup world, and lots of entrepreneurs are going for a piece of the action. Nothing in this book about Virtual Reality, Augmented Reality, or Fin-Tech is meant to be exhaustive, but we thought mentioning it as an identified growth area would be a good complement to The Manifesto's Observations and Forecast.

A few things have remained true since the Manifesto until now and those are:

- – No one seems to really question our web navigation Method or offer an alternative;
- – The users are still not asked what they want to see. Every Site, App, or software, offers a User Interface which the users accept and gets no choice upon;
- – Advertisements are becoming more and more annoying and increasingly intrusive, making the users very frustrated.

How do startups Start?

This is an interesting question. Seeing all the startups which come out with a product or a service and make it in front of our eyes, one may think that these companies magically become companies and that people achieve "Startup status" overnight. Actually, it is not usual for entrepreneurs to wake up as head of startup overnight...

The most typical (now mythical) scenario is the story of 2 cofounders who are the perfect pair. Long term friends, perfect complementarity of skills (usually business Vs. Tech), a garage in Palo Alto, lots of fast food, and two months of non-stop work buried in the garage.

Not only has this story been made famous by the Steve Jobs and Apple computer "most mythical garage startup" with Wozniak, but it has been duplicated and has actually happened many times over...

An argument could be made that this utopian brotherly type of perfect collaboration and groundbreaking innovation is still possible, but seldom does it play out that way... at least it would be safe to say the Startup Start has changed. I am not too familiar with the "old ways", but I would still want to maintain the "Garage dream scenario" as a reference of an ideal long lost.

Today, the race is a lot more frenetic. The gold rush mentality has spread wide amongst the youth. Access to technology (especially software) has become rather easy.

Combining that with Business interests from all industries coupled with the keen interest to stay on top of the digital trends, the result is pretty interesting.

On one side you now have an almost endless supply of "startups" fueled by several years of computer science development both in global business but simultaneously in academics.

Indeed, with computer science as one of the most enrolled courses across universities for the first time in history on the one side, and a lot bigger (virtually endless) pool of investors and interested groups to fuel the scene on the other side, the future promises to be promising!

The key equation is:

> **(Software ease + Cloud computing) x infrastructure access**
>
> **=**
>
> **democratization of software startups.**

The magical thing about the recent startups we see in the Silicon Valley and more and more around the world is that software developers are readily available combined with inexpensive cloud-based infrastructure like A.W.S, which allows for quick and easy app development and deployment in the cloud.

The fact is this: not only startups have been starting in a whole new way, but that way, is constantly morphing. Entrepreneurship is like a newborn. So many alarming signs could be normal, and the definition of normal is worthless, because, every enterprise gets to pave its own path and is a pioneer.

Although we cannot properly depict how startups start now, but we know it has changed a lot from before, and now that the latest gold rush and frenetic growth "in fear of missing out" has shaken down, we shall begin to see which models will sustain themselves

So, how do startups start today? Sometimes, you almost don't know anymore... with the development of apps and the democratization of Internet access through mobile devices, it has become very easy to build a startup around an app. There actually has been a massive flood of apps creation. Very few of them actually have a business (i.e. revenues) and each one of those failing apps, can be regarded as a failing startup...

That's a lot of startups...

Once Started, what do Startups do?

It may sound like a startup is great, but it is a business. So, obviously, like any business, we can assume people will try to make it work.

This is when (I am finding out) technology startups, especially software, are rather interesting.

The essence of the software (technology) business is, by nature, rather different.

It is always about Intellectual Property (IP).

Intellectual Property is if you want, a know-how, which you can turn into a product or a service, deliver it to consumers (users), and monetize on it.

Also important to highlight that it is needed to monetize ENOUGH.

The Startup Grind

So, here is a team with an idea to change the world. Different accounts somehow always relate the same story:

Set up the company, gather your people, establish work space, protocols, prototypes etc. and always, no matter what, there is always this need for funding.

Or is there…

It seems we (Startup-ers) are always coveting the ever more luring investments. Funding is synonym with success to most of us…

I once asked a VC why most starving entrepreneur dreaming to access an accelerator or incubator to receive $200,000 and give up 7% of her company. And why in the world would a previously funded company, many times over, that received millions if not hundreds of millions of venture money, STILL go for additional rounds of debt and equity funding?

You know what his answer was? It was good and thorough. He said it was about scaling and global growth worldwide. He explained how reserves are important. He also explained how expensive engineering can be, as well as legal fees (especially in certain cases) and infrastructure.

I understood his answer thoroughly in my intellect. But in my gut, I felt something was still wrong.

A company with the finances of multiple countries combined should be able to do whatever it needs to do to deliver its entrepreneurial promise, and create value, rather than further deepen its debt and dependency on creditors.

But, back then, I didn't know much. My question was genuine. I was looking at startups raising phenomenal amounts of money, to deliver a promise. To fulfill their dream and the dream of many; build the future…

However, most of them fail in this quest. The last optimist check showed about 80% failure.

The VC know this… all they need is 1 out of 20 to be well. And then 1 out of 100, to be a unicorn.

But let's get to a happy scenario.

Everyone's dream is about funding in the valley. It has always been. The industry of VC itself is needed in many cases, but the overall of HOW it has been happening, has shown some limits.

Although only 1 in a 100 Pitch to VCs may get a call to follow through, let's see how the relationship between Startup and VC happens.

When the Entrepreneur enters into contract with the investor, (especially institutional VC's) there are lots of sets of clauses which are setting the stage to the future relationships and the company sovereignty. We want to argue, after studying many of the documents, that most people involved in startups are unaware of the details involved in corporate management and equity implications.

Even within CEOs, probably only a selected few take the many hours needed to dig through the legalese and understand what the landscape in which you are leading your team and organization is. It is tough. After all the layers of corporate establishment in Delaware and registration in your home state (and the list is nice: Statement of information, bylaws, minutes, directors meetings, etc), there is all the HR stuff (contracts and relationships), and then, finally, you get to the sweetest part of this maze, which is the securities law.

The VC on their hand, have had ways of handling their Startup business for years. When you ask other business moguls like Warren Buffet about the startup investments, he baffles at the different rounds of funding like a very strange practice that he doesn't understand nor is interested in partaking in.

That was enlightening to me: Whatever everyone is doing, is just the way they know, or have learned. And now, as we (Humanity) are building and creating new things, we at STRAPDOOR, believe that it is also time for a new business model, where all interests align in a flexible and open manner, without borders.

A Business model that is actually powered by the cloud. An all integrative corporate structure that allows for the ultimate corporate governance. The following will be an attempt to consolidate years of observation in economics and human interactions.

The ideal has been searched for many years. We want to offer an attempt to present this ideological model which can only be brought about now, as software development becomes as cheap as it can, and global software development collaboration tools finally allow distributed teams to contribute from anywhere in the world, to the value creation.

The applications have always been very limited because of the physical and geographical nature of business this far. Now, with the new ways of creating value (software), we may need to evolve our thought process. This is where the introduction of the business model shall begin.

Capitalism is great. However, I don't say this like many people who have identified Capitalism as great system because it was the only alternative to Communism which was considered, by many, for a long time, as bad.

Capitalism is great for what it is. A Value driven model. Everything has value, and thus, we can begin to trade these different values. A degree of relativity makes the whole experiment amazing. But what if we have not fully thought through the relationship models that power society.

What is the definition of Value?

For centuries, all until recently, one of the foremost required condition for the exchange of value was the physical presence of 2 parties. Usually in a market or in any village / city where some kind of EXCHANGE happens, even with services.

With the development of software and the Internet, it is now possible to build value in new ways. There are not a 1000 ways of saying it, it's 1 word: software.

The Superiority of Software

A quick note on why software is superior to any other form of value is that, though very complex to establish and get used to, but once in place, SCALE is achievable. Your variable cost to distribute to 10 or 10, 000 000 is minimal If any. It is the power of digital content and the Internet. You can build a product on your laptop and get it into the hands of millions.

Value creation in Group

Scrum teaches us that software development is done in teams and communication tools allow better exchange of ideas to result into Wizardry by the Software Developers in order to turn those ideas into a responsive computer program.

CHAPTER 4. Mechanics of the business model

Contribution to the enterprise = Value
Value= Stock
Contribution to the enterprise =Stock

Initially, all contribution to the enterprise by the original developers and contributors are for stock only following vesting.

Very high return through buyback program locked in under conditions.

Example of conditions: company profits, timeline needed before repurchase, separation terms.

Excerpt from Stock purchase agreement (see exhibits at the end of this essay)

> (a) **Company Repurchase of Vested Shares.** The Shares shall not be transferrable at any time, to any party, and for any reason, except as set forth herein. Following the five (5)-year anniversary of the date that any Shares are released from forfeiture, such Shares may be repurchased from the Purchaser by the Company at a price of $0.1 per Share, *provided that*: the Company has reached annual profits of $10,000,000; and (iv) the Company determines, in its sole discretion, that such repurchase shall not adversely affect the Company's liquidity, business plan or financial health. The company determines that it will not purchase more 1,800,000 shares per year from the Purchaser. The company further may determine any more conditions that may be appropriate at the time to ensure sustainability of the share repurchase plan across the entire company

The general idea is to build an aggressive philosophy of contributors' ownership based on the following premise:

"If enough people have an incentive for something to do well, then it should indeed do well"

This is not meant meant to be a set in stone model, rather a new form of entrepreneurship model and company building method which aims at including all of the members/ contributors to the project, and including the users into the profits and growth of the company.

The buyback is subject to certain conditions that each company must establish for itself, what will work for it and will allow it to attract enough talent, and yet survive long enough until it reaches the success that every company aims at achieving.

It has been demonstrated that neither funding, debt, nor any kind of finances GUARANTEES the success of the enterprise, rather, we consistently see over 50% failure rate for funded tech companies.

Most Common Exits for companies that received Angel funding

Outcome	Percentage
Goes out of business	50.0
Sale to a larger company	20.0
Acqui-hire	15.0
Walking dead	7.0
Soft landing with a competitor	3.0
Bought out by a later investor	2.0
Bought out by a lifestyle entrepreneur	1.0
Becomes part of a roll-up	1.0
Disappears	0.9
Initial public offering (IPO)	0.1

(Source: http://blog.gust.com/the-startup-failure-rate-among-angel-funded-companies/)

We believe a new communitarian model would have equal chances, could be a lot funnier, and would maintain corporate sovereignty, allowing a possible longer life cycle to the entrepreneurial dream.

This applies mostly and only to hyper agile software in the cloud development startups.

Economics & Mechanics

- Management and fulfillment of the vision.

The covenant tool is used to instill hard anchored values which the founder wants to live and die by. The founding principles which the enterprise can be built upon.

For this business plan to work, the communitarian model must be subject to strict guidance and generous distribution of shares to many. It is in many ways counterintuitive to what can be thought anywhere. But it is the core of this business model we want to build. To ensure no interference or conflict of interests, the full control and decision making must be maintained in the hands of the one founder.

If you look at the stock ownership and control of top 500 companies, you will see that somehow surprisingly, very few interests/individuals/groups own most of these enterprises.

Acquisition of stock is the ultimate way for the enterprise to say: we are 1 team. If we win, you win too.

You know the best moment in entrepreneurship is when you give stock to others. You share a piece of this entrepreneurial dream with them, and just by that little gesture, we believe, you can create a feeling of belonging and community never reached before. And that's what we want to accomplish, and this essay is put out there as an internal corporate reference for us, but also for the world to stumble upon and maybe see a piece of this vision.

Though we are disclosing lots of internal mechanics we are using to build a company in this write-up, the information given here is only as a guiding tool for those who want to innovate in business modeling and build a communitarian business ecosystem.

- Company starts with large amount of shares with weight of voting stock all the way to non-voting stock (see example below) with the mission to distribute and give out the company to the world. Beginning with the Founder, team, and investors, everything is tied together by a buyback program in which the only way for the shares to be redeemed or transferred is through the company's BUYBACK program.

EXAMPLE:

1- **The Company has a total 22,222,222,222 Authorized shares.**
- 30% = Class C Preferred Voting Stock

- 30% = Class B Preferred Voting Stock
- 20% = Class A Preferred Voting Stock
- 20% = Class D Common Non-Voting stock

- Each class A voting stock vote weighs 2 times the vote of a Class B Voting Stock
- Each Class C voting stock vote weighs 10 times the vote of a Class A voting Stock

The par Value of the shares is $0.00001 / share

The high number of shares is intrinsically related to the long-term vision of the company to open its stock ownership to a large number of individuals over a period of time.

See exhibits at the end of this essay showing the example we used for the first establishment of such a model.

------------ A COMMUNITARIAN MODEL ------------

Phase 1: Establishment: 52% for founder: This is the step where the founder decides to establish his/her company and goes through the entire diligence of business establishment, incorporation, bylaws creation (see covenant) and consolidation of the vision and objectives of the company.

This should ensure beyond full control of the company and protection of sovereignty for the life of the company.

Phase 2: Growth and Development: 12% for the Team: This is where the founder brings on talent to start building the vision. That is, technical skills, developers, and business development. Limited amount should be open to the team yearly, based on the need and growth of the company. As the company builds value, there should be an increase in the value of the stock and the company can be offering progressively lower amount of shares to the contributors, all the while increasing the value of the stock.

Phase 3: Scale: 20%: Once the team has built some value into the company, has a working prototype, and/or some users, the company can make some non-voting stock available to Investors who want to support the enterprise.

Lastly, once the core team and investors are on board, and the company launches a product that people can use, benefit from, and buy; in time, the company shall begin to offer stock to a certain limited and restricted class of its users, using the only mechanism we could find in the economic system through gifting of shares to a certain limited and restricted class of paying customers. Based on the information we obtained from the Security and Exchange Commission attorney who confirmed: "If you are a beer company, you can gift a share to every customer that buys a case of beer from you."

There lies what we believe is the key ingredient and missing piece in the global puzzle of communities coming together. It resides in the gift. The gift of business ownership to the world. One company's aim should be to become large enough to share with others. Of course, if you may not agree with this economic philosophy, it is okay. But, for the record, it is a possible path. And the one we choose to follow and spearhead in the chaos of entrepreneurship.

Phase 4: Rooting: 16% for users. This is once there is a solid platform / product built that has gained enough traction to grow into a profitable solution for the users. At that point, a special tier of users gets to participate in the share ownership buyback program through receiving gifted stock for their purchases.

We propose a different paradigm where the founder retains all the control to see through the communitarian vision of his enterprise. It comes at a high weight of responsibility, but the founder becomes more of a catalyst to the input of everyone else... Will he make mistakes? Sure, but as long as he retains his sovereignty, he should aim at the best possible outcome for the enterprise, his creation... Our paradigm does not believe in getting rid of a founder & replace him/her by outside appointed CEOs (referred to certain prominent figures as "professional CEOs").

We don't think it actually increases the long term likelihood of success of an enterprise. It makes no sense. This idea of a professional CEO seems rather useful to someone who owns a lots of different companies and needs another employee to do a job. Not necessarily live the dream of entrepreneurship. There are countless examples - not going to be mentioned here- where firing the founder did not actually help the enterprise. Notorious VC's are now trying hard to keep the founding team on board as they realized no outside "professional" can have the burning desire of the founders, regardless of their shortfalls... Aren't we all humans?

A CEO should be a founder. Or to say, the founder should be the CEO. Of course to a certain level "more handholding" may be necessary. But I truly think it all depends on the corporate establishment and structure of the company. The whole concept of "Adult Supervision" is okay, and I think very valuable, but when it translates into "getting rid of the founders" I think the protocols should be a little more in favor of the founder CEO than anyone else within the enterprise. (RIP Steve Jobs. Thank you for teaching by example).
The Founder, may choose to appoint a CEO other than himself, but all the while maintaining full control to see through the communitarian model he/she would have committed to whole heartedly.
Without a solid business structure that protects the sovereignty of the enterprise to fulfill its commitment to the communitarian model, there will be people whose greed will tempt them to dispatch the equity otherwise or sell out...

- **A communitarian Model.**

Open source teaches us that we can contribute and create value for the world and actually solve important problems that definitely empower humanity to reach further into the nascent Digital Revolution* (ref to manifesto).

I think it is safe to say most companies reason primarily in terms of employees... where HIRING and EMPLOYEE BENEFITS remain the norm. A few owners and lots of executants.

You see, retention efforts and employee benefits with astronomical pay are just an indirect way of recognizing that, at last, the know-how of the WORKER is appreciated because we are bending over backward for you to make the stuff we need. (Yes, this is addressed to you hackers and inventors who got into the corporate 9-5). There is a recognition of this trend, which I was happy to catch a recent interview by renowned VC Chamath Palihapitiya from Social Capital (Chamath if you read this, send me a msg).

Critical Mass of CS and Developers: A new ERA.

Developers are now entering a new Era. The hordes of CS graduates which will be flooding the market will drive the value and cost of development down, but simultaneously, there will be so many more ideas and the need for development, as all the barriers to starting a software enterprise lessen.

Another interesting point will be when everyone finally gets the clue that, in Silicon Valley "Software is Eating the world". In essence, everything will be software or operating with software.

Our focus and interest remain in applications and software that is made for the masses. Think of the best 5 Apps or programs ever made. Anyone could use them and benefit from them: Communication, GPS, Commerce, Games, etc.

To summarize:

This new business model is described as Communitarian.

Strapdoor, Inc. is the first company to implement it and build a company and a team around it.

We detail the share split strategy used for STRAPDOOR as well as some key elements that must be implemented to ensure the continuation of the enterprise.

A few elements must be in place:

It is very important to maintain full control within the hands of one sole person so as to

15

avoid break up points where a difference between two co-founders or founders and investors puts the team and company in jeopardy.

The key elements of this model are embedded in the bylaws. The founder must remain in control and be adamant about fulfilling the vision of a communitarian enterprise, where he studies, understands, and utilizes the equity distribution ability the company has to foster a new culture of entrepreneurship.

Important to note is that most traditional investors and institutional bodies *will not like this model*, as it aims to offer a counter model to the current, and well-established models, which have been in place for the last 50 years- If you are a VC reading this and disagree, contact us through our investor portal –

Our study of the current ways made us realize that it is all to the benefit of the VC's and existing powers, rather than to the benefit of the entrepreneurs and startups.

Although the small equity given in the first round of investment may seem worth it to a starving entrepreneur, the loss of sovereignty that comes with the acceptance of that investment is the biggest opportunity cost many startup founders don't take into account.

The VC gives money with the underlying plan to have the startup run out of money and need to raise funds again. Each step is called a Serie. From the Angel round to the Series A, then B, then C, etc. every additional round, though on paper shows an increase in the global value of the enterprise, but truly, what it does is confer more and more power to the investors/board while diluting the founders.

Different founders have put in place different strategies to counter this dilution, but, ultimately, either after a certain amount OR a certain time, the founder will lose his ability to decide and control the company he started.

It is also important to acknowledge that as long as the founder follows and serves the interests of the higher powers that be, there may be no need to replace them. When, however, a founder's vision or goals, clash with those of the investors (who often represent different interests), the "ousting" protocol is built into the very first set of documents signed between the company and the investors.

Our communitarian model, aims at offering an alternative to this method of startup building. We fuse crowdsourcing, open sourcing, and community ownership models.

Also important to note is that only very few companies will be able to carry on this plan to the end, and it will present plenty of challenges. This model requires many great contributors and developers, to embrace the vision of a communitarian enterprise, with a long-term return plan, as there will be no immediate salaries or benefits from the stock ownership until the company reaches key milestones.

The stock philosophy here aims at offering layers of packages to the participants, starting with most aggressive to less aggressive as the team grows.

It is up to the founder to engineer the model and set the triggering milestones for the buyback plan.

In our case, we set the time to: not before 5 years, and not before 10 million dollars in profits.

The strategy is to bring together talented individuals that will contribute similarly to an open source project, but for actual becoming part of the SD enterprise, receiving stock in exchange for their contributions. The fundamental premise is that the value created through the contributions will eventually attract some investors that will buy into the buyback plan and infuse cash into the growth stages, allowing the company to pay full-time wages to a few key members of the full-time management and operations team, while the very majority of contributors will remain freelancers, independent contractors, claiming tasks as they want and progressively building further the software.

This model can only be applied to software development as the barriers to entry in hardware or other technology segments do indeed require tremendous amounts of cash.

We see in this software revolution and democratization, a way to harness the power of the community to build value in a whole new way.

The key element here is for the company, through its founder's control, to remain fully independent from outside pressures and influences, and keep the developments going in the set direction, while protecting the intellectual property from falling into the hands of other interest groups.

One of the tools used in order to accomplish this, is to begin the company with a set large amount of authorized shares, which will be distributed over a period of time to the different incumbents (founder, team, investors, and eventually users). The company also will not authorize more shares at all, at any time. This is the only way to ensure non-dilution of ownership.

In addition, to structure the control of the company, some of the stock must be given a lot more weight than other stocks so as to ensure retention of control all the while permitting a wide distribution of the stock. Lastly, for the buyback program to work for many, the profits milestone must be big enough to permit the distribution to the many.

In essence, by repurchasing the shares, the company creates a recurring cycle that will allow it in time to re-issue more shares to more contributors, spreading the wealth it is creating to the people that enable it.

The founder's big chunk of ownership in the beginning, once bought back by the company should be recycled in the user pool of shares, ending in the users owning a big part of the company stock, while keeping the control within the hands of the founder thanks to the retention of the controlling share of the total stock (thanks to the weight of the shares).

17

It is worth noting that the recycling perspectives which such a model allows by repurchasing the shares year after year, the company should be able to re-issue more shares to new incumbents- team, investors, but most importantly, users. At that point, the founder would have received plenty of profits from the company to live a comfortable life and can then focus on growing the company's reach and business growth, which will translate into benefits for many people, including team members (contributors), investors, and (unique to this model), the users as well.

The numbers can be played with and further engineered by each company/ founder team, to determine the split, timelines and other parameters that can be customized at will (after proper legal counsel). Within this model, we believe, lies the beginning of a new wave of entrepreneurship that can reach deeper than anything else before in the modern economy, because of the 2 simple factors:

UNITY OF PURPOSE – COMMONALITY OF BENEFITS

A Note on perpetuity:

With the recycling ability which this model offers, a founder could establish a trust to run his controlling ownership post-mortem allowing to ensure the fulfillment of the goals and continuation of this model theoretically forever, as long as the work realized in his/her lifetime establishes the company as a valuable enough proposition, for enough people, to allow sustainability of business operations and enough profits to carry on.

Please refer to attached exhibits that will complete the documentation of this model as it is today at the end of 2016. Hopefully, some will pick up on it, and build many businesses in the same sense, allowing for the democratization of ownership of the only and most powerful tool existing in our Capitalistic system: The shares of a Corporation. We believe it's the way to the future. Join us. www.strapdoor.info

In Tech. We Are Here to Serve,

Please note: All materials have been prepared for general information purposes only to permit you to learn more about our firm, our services and our experience in the business model building. The information presented is not legal advice, is not to be acted on as such, may not be current and is subject to change without notice.

Exhibits: Start up establishment and relationship contracts for communitarian model.

Exhibit Zero: Table of Content

-----EXHIBIT 1. Stock purchase agreement-----

_____, INC.

RESTRICTED STOCK PURCHASE AGREEMENT ESPECIALLY PREPARED FOR

This Restricted Stock Purchase Agreement (the "Agreement") is made as of_____, 2016 by and between _____, Inc., a Delaware corporation (the "Company"), and _____ ("Purchaser"). The Company's plans to operate as a technology company.

TERM/EXPIRATION: This Stock purchase agreement is intended to be exercised by the Purchaser as soon as practicable, after obtaining necessary counsel, and shall cease to be exercisable 40 days after the Date it is offered.

2.   **Sale of Stock**. Subject to the terms and conditions of this Agreement, on the Purchase Date (as defined below) the Company will issue and sell to Purchaser, and Purchaser agrees to purchase from the Company_____ **Class B (the "Shares") at a purchase price of _____per Share for a total purchase price of _____.** The term "Shares" refers to the purchased Shares and all securities received in replacement of or in connection with the Shares pursuant to stock dividends or splits, all securities received in replacement of the Shares in a recapitalization, merger, reorganization, exchange or the like, and all new, substituted or additional securities or other properties to which Purchaser is entitled by reason of Purchaser's ownership of the Shares.

3.   **Purchase.** The purchase and sale of the Shares under this Agreement shall occur at the principal office of the Company simultaneously with the execution and

delivery of this Agreement by the parties or on such other date as the Company and Purchaser shall agree (the "Purchase Date"). As soon as practicable following the Purchase Date, the Company will deliver to Purchaser a certificate representing the Shares to be purchased by Purchaser (which shall be issued in Purchaser's name) against payment of the purchase price therefor by Purchaser by (a) check made payable to the Company, (b) cancellation of indebtedness of the Company to Purchaser, (c) services previously rendered by Purchaser to the Company, or (d) by a combination of the foregoing. The Company shall issue the Shares to Purchaser by entering such Shares in Purchaser's name as of such date in the books and records of the Company or, if applicable, a duly authorized transfer agent of the Company, against payment of the purchase price therefor by Purchaser.

4. **Limitations on Transfer**. In addition to any other limitation on transfer created by applicable securities laws, Purchaser shall not assign, encumber or dispose of any interest in the Shares while the Shares are subject to the Company's Repurchase Option (as defined below). After any Shares have been released from the Repurchase Option, Purchaser shall not assign, encumber or dispose of any interest in such Shares except in compliance with the provisions below and applicable securities laws.

(a)   **Repurchase Option**.

(i)   In the event of the voluntary or involuntary termination of Purchaser's Continuous Service Status (as defined below) for any reason (including death or Disability (as defined below)), with or without cause, the Company shall upon the date of such termination (the "Termination Date") have an irrevocable, exclusive option (the "Repurchase Option") for a period of 6 months from such date to repurchase all or any portion of the Shares held by Purchaser as of the Termination Date which have not yet been released from the Company's Repurchase Option for the par value price of those Shares as in the Articles of Incorporation.

(ii)   Unless the Company notifies Purchaser within 6 months from the Termination Date that it does not intend to exercise its Repurchase Option with respect to some or all of the Shares, the Repurchase Option shall be deemed automatically exercised by the Company as of the end of such 6-month period following such Termination Date, provided that the Company may notify Purchaser that it is exercising its Repurchase Option as of a date prior to the end of such 6-month period. Unless Purchaser is otherwise notified by the Company pursuant to the preceding sentence that the Company does not intend to exercise its Repurchase Option as to some or all of the Shares to which it applies at the time of termination, execution of this Agreement by Purchaser constitutes written notice to Purchaser of the Company's intention to exercise its Repurchase Option with respect to all Shares to which such Repurchase Option applies. The Company, at its choice, may satisfy its payment obligation to Purchaser with respect to exercise of the Repurchase Option by either (A) delivering a check to Purchaser in the amount of the purchase price for the Shares being

20

repurchased, or (B) in the event Purchaser is indebted to the Company, canceling an amount of such indebtedness equal to the purchase price for the Shares being repurchased, or (C) by a combination of (A) and (B) so that the combined payment and cancellation of indebtedness equals such purchase price. In the event of any deemed automatic exercise of the Repurchase Option pursuant to this Section 3(a)(i) in which Purchaser is indebted to the Company, such indebtedness equal to the purchase price of the Shares being repurchased shall be deemed automatically canceled as of the end of the 6-month period following the Termination Date unless the Company otherwise satisfies its payment obligations. As a result of any repurchase of Shares pursuant to this Section 3(a), the Company shall become the legal and beneficial owner of the Shares being repurchased and shall have all rights and interest therein or related thereto, and the Company shall have the right to transfer to its own name the number of Shares being repurchased by the Company, without further action by Purchaser.

(iii)   All of the Shares shall initially be subject to the Repurchase Option (the "Vesting Shares"). One fifth (1/5th) of the Vesting Shares shall be released from the Repurchase Option on each anniversary of your reception of this restricted purchase agreement period, either January or July, until all Vesting Shares are released from the Repurchase Option.   Any releases from the Repurchase Option shall immediately cease as of the Termination Date. Fractional shares shall be rounded to the nearest whole share.

(b)   **Company Repurchase of Vested Shares.** The Shares shall not be transferrable at any time, to any party, and for any reason, except as set forth herein. Following the five (5)-year anniversary of the date that any Shares are released from forfeiture, such Shares may be repurchased from the Purchaser by the Company at a price of $0.1 per Share, *provided that*: the Company has reached annual profits of $10,000,000; and (iv) the Company determines, in its sole discretion, that such repurchase shall not adversely affect the Company's liquidity, business plan or financial health. The company determines that it will not purchase more 1,800,000 shares per year from the Purchaser. The company further may determine any more conditions that may be appropriate at the time to ensure sustainability of the share repurchase plan across the entire company

(i)   **Exception for Certain Family Transfers**. Anything to the contrary contained in this Section 3(b) notwithstanding, the transfer of any or all of the Shares during Purchaser's lifetime or on Purchaser's death by will or intestacy to Purchaser's Immediate Family or a trust for the benefit of Purchaser or Purchaser's Immediate Family shall be exempt from the provisions of this Section 3(b). "Immediate Family" as used herein shall mean lineal descendant or antecedent, spouse (or spouse's antecedents), father, mother, brother or sister (or their descendants), stepchild (or their antecedents or descendants), aunt or uncle (or their antecedents or descendants), brother-in-law or sister-in-law (or their antecedents or descendants) and shall include adoptive relationships, or any person sharing the Purchaser's household (other than a

21

tenant or an employee). In such case, the transferee or other recipient shall receive and hold the Shares so transferred subject to the provisions of this Section, and there shall be no further transfer of such Shares except in accordance with the terms of this Section 3.

(c) **Company's Right to Purchase upon Involuntary Transfer.** In the event, at any time after the date of this Agreement, of any transfer by operation of law or other involuntary transfer (including divorce or death, but excluding in the event of death a transfer to Immediate Family as set forth in Section 3(b)(i) above of all or a portion of the Shares by the record holder thereof, the Company shall have the right to purchase all of the Shares transferred for a symbolic $100. The purchaser acknowledges that in case of separation, all unvested shares are being relinquished and sold back to the company for par value

(d) **Assignment.** The right of the Company to purchase any part of the Shares may be assigned in whole or in part to any holder or holders of capital stock of the Company or other persons or organizations.

(e) **Restrictions Binding on Transferees.** All transferees of Shares or any interest therein will receive and hold such Shares or interest subject to the provisions of this Agreement, including, insofar as applicable, the Repurchase Option. Any sale or transfer of the Shares shall be void unless the provisions of this Agreement are satisfied.

(f) **Continuation of Rights:** The first right of refusal granted to the company in Section 3(b) and 3(c) above shall continue In the event of an IPO, upon the first sale of Common Stock of the Company to the general public pursuant to a registration statement filed with and declared effective by the Securities and Exchange Commission under the Securities Act of 1933, as amended (the "Securities Act"). Upon such an event, the Company will remove any appropriate notices on the certificates and a new certificate or certificates representing the Shares not repurchased shall be issued, on request, without the said legend(s).

(g) **Lock-up Agreement.** In connection with the initial public offering of the Company's securities, the company maintains a first right of refusal to the sale of any share and the Company should be made aware in writing of any intent to sell by the Purchaser. In addition, upon request of the Company or the underwriters managing such offering of the Company's securities, Purchaser hereby agrees not to sell, make any short sale of, loan, grant any option for the purchase of, or otherwise dispose of any securities of the Company (other than those included in the registration) without the prior written consent of the Company or such underwriters, as the case may be, for such period of time (not to exceed 180 days) from the effective date of such registration as may be requested by the Company or such managing underwriters and to execute an agreement reflecting the foregoing as may be requested by the underwriters at the time of the Company's initial public offering. In addition, upon request of the Company or the underwriters managing a public offering of the Company's securities (other than the initial public offering), Purchaser hereby agrees to be bound by similar restrictions, and to sign a similar agreement, in connection with no more than one additional registration statement filed within 12 months after the closing date of the initial public offering, provided that the duration of the lock-up period with respect to such additional registration shall not exceed 90 days from the effective date of such additional registration statement. Notwithstanding the foregoing, if during the last 17 days of the restricted period, the Company issues an earnings release or material news or a material event relating to the Company occurs, or prior to the expiration of the restricted period the Company announces that it will release earnings results during the 16-day period beginning on the last day of the restricted period, then, upon the request of the managing underwriter, to the extent required by any FINRA rules, the restrictions imposed by this subsection shall continue to apply until the end of the third trading day following the expiration of the 15-day period beginning on the issuance of the earnings release or the occurrence of the material news or material event. In no event will the restricted period extend beyond 216 days after the effective date of the registration statement.

5.   **Escrow of Unvested Shares.** For purposes of facilitating the enforcement of the provisions of Section 3 above, Purchaser agrees, immediately upon receipt of the certificate(s) for the Shares subject to the Repurchase Option, to deliver such certificate(s), together with an Assignment Separate from Certificate in the form attached to this Agreement as Exhibit A executed by Purchaser and by Purchaser's spouse (if required for transfer), in blank, to the Secretary of the Company, or the Secretary's designee, to hold such certificate(s) and Assignment Separate from Certificate in escrow and to take all such actions and to effectuate all such transfers and/or releases as are in accordance with the terms of this Agreement. Purchaser hereby acknowledges that the Secretary of the Company, or the Secretary's designee, is so appointed as the escrow holder with the foregoing authorities as a material inducement to make this Agreement and that said appointment is coupled with an interest and is accordingly irrevocable. Purchaser agrees that said escrow holder shall not be liable to any party hereof (or to any other party). The escrow holder may rely upon any letter, notice or other document executed by any signature purported to be genuine and may resign at any time. Purchaser agrees that if the Secretary of the Company, or the Secretary's designee, resigns as escrow holder for any or no reason, the Board of Directors of the Company shall have the power to appoint a successor to serve as escrow holder pursuant to the terms of this Agreement.

6.   **Investment and Taxation Representations.** In connection with the purchase of the Shares, Purchaser represents to the Company the following:

(a)   Purchaser is aware of the Company's business affairs and financial condition and has acquired sufficient information about the Company to reach an informed and knowledgeable decision to acquire the Shares. Purchaser is purchasing the Shares for investment for Purchaser's own account only and not with a view to, or for resale in connection with, any "distribution" thereof within the meaning of the Securities

23

Act or under any applicable provision of state law. Purchaser does not have any present intention to transfer the Shares to any other person or entity.

(b)   Purchaser understands that the Shares have not been registered under the Securities Act by reason of a specific exemption therefrom, which exemption depends upon, among other things, the bona fide nature of Purchaser's investment intent as expressed herein.

(c)   Purchaser further acknowledges and understands that the securities must be held indefinitely unless they are subsequently registered under the Securities Act or an exemption from such registration is available. Purchaser further acknowledges and understands that the Company is under no obligation to register the securities.

(d)   Purchaser is familiar with the provisions of Rules 144 and 701, each promulgated under the Securities Act, which, in substance, permit limited public resale of "restricted securities" acquired, directly or indirectly, from the issuer of the securities (or from an affiliate of such issuer), in a non-public offering subject to the satisfaction of certain conditions. Purchaser understands that the Company provides no assurances as to whether he or she will be able to resell any or all of the Shares pursuant to Rule 144 or Rule 701, which rules require, among other things, that resales of securities take place only after the holder of the Shares has held the Shares for certain specified time periods, and under certain circumstances, that certain information about the Company be current and publicly available, and that resales of securities be limited in volume and take place only pursuant to brokered transactions. Notwithstanding this Section 5(d), Purchaser acknowledges and agrees to the restrictions set forth in Section 5(e) below.

(e)   Purchaser further understands that in the event all of the applicable requirements of Rule 144 or 701 are not satisfied, registration under the Securities Act, compliance with Regulation A, or some other registration exemption will be required; and that, notwithstanding the fact that Rules 144 and 701 are not exclusive, the Staff of the Securities and Exchange Commission has expressed its opinion that persons proposing to sell private placement securities other than in a registered offering and otherwise than pursuant to Rule 144 or 701 will have a substantial burden of proof in establishing that an exemption from registration is available for such offers or sales, and that such persons and their respective brokers who participate in such transactions do so at their own risk.

(f)   Purchaser understands that Purchaser may suffer adverse tax consequences as a result of Purchaser's purchase or disposition of the Shares. Purchaser represents that Purchaser has consulted any tax consultants Purchaser deems advisable in connection with the purchase or disposition of the Shares and that Purchaser is not relying on the Company for any tax advice.

(g)   Purchaser further acknowledges and understands that there are no claims made whatsoever by the Company on potential gains, revenues, or profits to be made, and that the fulfillment of the conditions outlined in 3(b) which will allow the

24

company to purchase the shares back are not a guarantee. Those conditions as well as any other conditions outlined in any document are only given as optimistic projections on what can be achieved and that, as in any venture, the outcome will depend on a variety of elements which the Company cannot guarantee. The purchaser acknowledges that he/she will seek proper counsel before committing to this and any contracts to be entered in with the company and is given sufficient time to seek all counsel and conduct all diligence relating to the relationship with the company. The purchaser agrees to hold the company harmful of all claims pertaining to Investment and taxation representations and has collected all information available today as to the potentials and risks of the Company.

7.   **Restrictive Legends and Stop-Transfer Orders.**

(a)   **Legends.** Any certificate or certificates representing the Shares shall bear the following legends (as well as any legends required by applicable state and federal corporate and securities laws):

(i)   "THE SECURITIES REPRESENTED HEREBY HAVE NOT BEEN REGISTERED UNDER THE SECURITIES ACT OF 1933, AND HAVE BEEN ACQUIRED FOR INVESTMENT AND NOT WITH A VIEW TO, OR IN CONNECTION WITH, THE SALE OR DISTRIBUTION THEREOF. NO SUCH SALE OR DISTRIBUTION MAY BE EFFECTED WITHOUT AN EFFECTIVE REGISTRATION STATEMENT RELATED THERETO OR AN OPINION OF COUNSEL IN A FORM SATISFACTORY TO THE COMPANY THAT SUCH REGISTRATION IS NOT REQUIRED UNDER THE SECURITIES ACT OF 1933."

(ii)   "THE SHARES REPRESENTED BY THIS CERTIFICATE MAY BE TRANSFERRED ONLY IN ACCORDANCE WITH THE TERMS OF AN AGREEMENT BETWEEN THE COMPANY AND THE STOCKHOLDER, A COPY OF WHICH IS ON FILE WITH AND MAY BE OBTAINED FROM THE SECRETARY OF THE COMPANY."

(iii)   Any legend required to be placed thereon by the California Commissioner of Corporations OR the purchaser's state of residence Commissioner of Corporations.

(b)   **Stop-Transfer Notices.** Purchaser agrees that, in order to ensure compliance with the restrictions referred to herein, the Company may issue appropriate "stop transfer" instructions to its transfer agent, if any, and that, if the Company transfers its own securities, it may make appropriate notations to the same effect in its own records.

(c)   **Refusal to Transfer.** The Company shall not be required (i) to transfer on its books any Shares that have been sold or otherwise transferred in violation of any of the provisions of this Agreement or (ii) to treat as owner of such Shares or to accord the right to vote or pay dividends to any purchaser or other transferee to whom such Shares shall have been so transferred.

8. **No Employment Rights.** Nothing in this Agreement shall affect in any manner whatsoever the right or power of the Company, or a Parent or Subsidiary of the Company, to terminate Purchaser's employment, consulting, or contractual relationship, for any reason, with or without cause.

9. **Section 83(b) Election.** Purchaser understands that Section 83(a) of the Internal Revenue Code of 1986, as amended (the "Code"), taxes as ordinary income the difference between the amount paid for the Shares and the fair market value of the Shares as of the date any restrictions on the Shares lapse. In this context, "restriction" means the right of the Company to buy back the Shares pursuant to the Repurchase Option set forth in Section 3(a) of this Agreement. Purchaser understands that Purchaser may elect to be taxed at the time the Shares are purchased, rather than when and as the Repurchase Option expires, by filing an election under Section 83(b) (an "83(b) Election") of the Code with the Internal Revenue Service within 30 days from the date of purchase. Even if the fair market value of the Shares at the time of the execution of this Agreement equals the amount paid for the Shares, the election must be made to avoid income under Section 83(a) in the future. Purchaser understands that failure to file such an election in a timely manner may result in adverse tax consequences for Purchaser. Purchaser further understands that an additional copy of such election form should be filed with Purchaser's federal income tax return for the calendar year in which the date of this Agreement falls. Purchaser acknowledges that the foregoing is only a summary of the effect of United States federal income taxation with respect to purchase of the Shares hereunder, does not purport to be complete, and is not intended or written to be used, and cannot be used, for the purposes of avoiding taxpayer penalties. Purchaser further acknowledges that the Company has directed Purchaser to seek independent advice regarding the applicable provisions of the Code, the income tax laws of any municipality, state or foreign country in which Purchaser may reside, and the tax consequences of Purchaser's death.

Purchaser agrees that he will execute and deliver to the Company with this executed Agreement a copy of the Acknowledgment and Statement of Decision Regarding Section 83(b) Election (the "Acknowledgment"), attached hereto as Exhibit B. Purchaser further agrees that Purchaser will execute and submit with the Acknowledgment a copy of the 83(b) Election, attached hereto as Exhibit C, if Purchaser has indicated in the Acknowledgment Purchaser's decision to make such an election.

10. **Certain Defined Terms.**

(a) **"Consultant"** means any person, including an advisor but not an Employee, who is engaged by the Company to render services (other than capital-raising services) and is compensated for such services, and any Director whether compensated for such services or not.

(b) **"Continuous Service Status"** means the absence of any interruption or termination of service as an Employee or Consultant. Continuous Service Status as an Employee or Consultant shall not be considered interrupted or terminated in the case of: (i) Company approved sick leave; (ii) military leave; (iii) any other bona fide leave of absence approved by the Company, provided that such leave is for a period of not more than ninety (90) days, unless reemployment upon the expiration of such leave is guaranteed by contract or statute, or unless provided otherwise pursuant to a written Company policy. Also, Continuous Service Status as an Employee or Consultant shall not be considered interrupted or terminated in the case of a transfer between locations of the Company or its successor, or a change in status from an Employee to a Consultant or from a Consultant to an Employee.

(c) **"Director"** means a member of the Board of Directors of the Company.

(d) **"Employee"** means any person employed by the Company with the status of employment determined pursuant to such factors as are deemed appropriate by the Board of Directors of the Company in its sole discretion, subject to any requirements of applicable laws, including the Code. The payment by the Company of a director's fee shall not be sufficient to constitute "employment" of such director by the Company.

11. **Miscellaneous**.

(a) **Governing Law**. This Agreement and all acts and transactions pursuant hereto and the rights and obligations of the parties hereto shall be governed, construed and interpreted in accordance with the laws of the State of California, without giving effect to principles of conflicts of law.

(b) **Entire Agreement; Enforcement of Rights**. This Agreement sets forth the entire agreement and understanding of the parties relating to the subject matter herein and merges all prior discussions between them. **All prior documents, conversations, proposals, negotiations, ideas, or representations are made void by this agreement.** No modification of or amendment to this Agreement, nor any waiver of any rights under this Agreement, shall be effective unless in writing signed by the parties to this Agreement. The failure by either party to enforce any rights under this Agreement shall not be construed as a waiver of any rights of such party.

(c) **Severability**. If one or more provisions of this Agreement are held to be unenforceable under applicable law, the parties agree to renegotiate such provision in good faith. In the event that the parties cannot reach a mutually agreeable and enforceable replacement for such provision, then (i) such provision shall be excluded from this Agreement, (ii) the balance of the Agreement shall be interpreted as if such provision were so excluded and (iii) the balance of the Agreement shall be enforceable in accordance with its terms.

27

(d) **Construction**. This Agreement is the result of negotiations between and has been reviewed by each of the parties hereto and their respective counsel, if any; accordingly, this Agreement shall be deemed to be the product of all of the parties hereto, and no ambiguity shall be construed in favor of or against any one of the parties hereto.

(e) **Notices**. Any notice required or permitted by this Agreement shall be in writing and shall be deemed sufficient upon delivery, when delivered personally or by overnight courier or sent by email or fax (upon customary confirmation of receipt), or forty-eight (48) hours after being deposited in the U.S. mail as certified or registered mail with postage prepaid, addressed to the party to be notified at such party's address or fax number as set forth on the signature page or as subsequently modified by written notice.

(f) **Counterparts**. This Agreement may be executed in two or more counterparts, each of which shall be deemed an original and all of which together shall constitute one instrument.

(g) **Successors and Assigns**. The rights and benefits of this Agreement shall inure to the benefit of, and be enforceable by the Company's successors and assigns. The rights and obligations of Purchaser under this Agreement may only be assigned with the prior written consent of the Company.

(h) **Electronic Delivery**. The Company may, in its sole discretion, decide to deliver any documents related to this Agreement by electronic means. Purchaser hereby consents to receive such documents by electronic delivery and agrees to participate through an on-line or electronic system established and maintained by the Company or a third party designated by the Company.

(i) **California Corporate Securities Law**. THE SALE OF THE SECURITIES WHICH ARE THE SUBJECT OF THIS AGREEMENT HAS NOT BEEN QUALIFIED WITH THE COMMISSIONER OF CORPORATIONS OF THE STATE OF CALIFORNIA AND THE ISSUANCE OF THE SECURITIES OR THE PAYMENT OR RECEIPT OF ANY PART OF THE CONSIDERATION THEREFOR PRIOR TO THE QUALIFICATION IS UNLAWFUL, UNLESS THE SALE OF SECURITIES IS EXEMPT FROM QUALIFICATION BY SECTION 25100, 25102 OR 25105 OF THE DELAWARE CORPORATIONS CODE. THE RIGHTS OF ALL PARTIES TO THIS AGREEMENT ARE EXPRESSLY CONDITIONED UPON THE QUALIFICATION BEING OBTAINED, UNLESS THE SALE IS SO EXEMPT.

Out of state additional requirements: IF purchaser is not a California resident, additional documents and/or exemption documents may be required to sign and be added to this agreement as amendments to satisfy local state laws. Al purchasers must ensure they are doing their diligence to ensure the individual compliance with state and federal laws. The purchaser agrees to swiftly return any amendments or additional documents

within 5 days of written request by the "Company" so as to maintain the integrity of this agreement.
[Signature Page Follows]

The parties have executed this Agreement as of the date first set forth above.

THE COMPANY:

_____,INC.

By:_____
(Signature)

Name: _____
Title: CEO, Director.

Address: _____

PURCHASER:

Advice of Counsel. I ACKNOWLEDGE THAT, IN EXECUTING THIS AGREEMENT, I HAVE HAD THE OPPORTUNITY TO SEEK THE ADVICE OF INDEPENDENT LEGAL COUNSEL, AND I HAVE READ AND UNDERSTOOD ALL OF THE TERMS AND PROVISIONS OF THIS AGREEMENT. THIS AGREEMENT SHALL NOT BE CONSTRUED AGAINST ANY PARTY BY REASON OF THE DRAFTING OR PREPARATION HEREOF.

Name:_____
(Signature)

Address:_____

_____

_____

Date:_____

EXHIBIT A

ASSIGNMENT SEPARATE FROM CERTIFICATE

Instructions: *Please do not fill in any blanks other than the signature line. The purpose of this assignment is to enable the Company to exercise its repurchase option set forth in the Agreement without requiring additional signatures on the part of Purchaser.*

     FOR VALUE RECEIVED and pursuant to that certain Restricted Stock Purchase Agreement between the undersigned ("Purchaser") and _____, Inc., a Delaware corporation (the "Company"), dated _____ (the "Agreement"), Purchaser hereby sells, assigns and transfers unto the Company _____ (_____) Class A shares of Company stock standing in Purchaser's name on the Company's books and represented by Certificate No. _____, and does hereby irrevocably constitute and appoint _____ to transfer said stock on the books of the Company with full power of substitution in the premises. THIS ASSIGNMENT MAY ONLY BE USED AS AUTHORIZED BY THE AGREEMENT AND THE EXHIBITS THERETO.

Dated:_____   PURCHASER:

                                   _____
                                   (Signature)

                                   Address:

                                   _____
                                   _____

                                   _____
                                   Spouse of Purchaser (if applicable)

EXHIBIT B

ACKNOWLEDGMENT AND STATEMENT
OF DECISION REGARDING SECTION 83(b) ELECTION

Instructions: *Please determine whether Purchaser will make an 83(b) election for the Shares, and have Purchaser fill out this form and provide Company with a copy.*

The undersigned has entered into a stock purchase agreement with_____Inc., a Delaware corporation (the "Company"), pursuant to which the undersigned is purchasing _____shares of Class ____stock of the Company (the "Shares"). In connection with the purchase of the Shares, the undersigned hereby represents as follows:

1.   The undersigned has carefully reviewed the stock purchase agreement pursuant to which the undersigned is purchasing the Shares.

2.   The undersigned either [check and complete as applicable]:

(a) ___has consulted, and has been fully advised by, the undersigned's own tax advisor, _____, whose business address is _____, regarding the federal, state and local tax consequences of purchasing the Shares, and particularly regarding the advisability of making elections pursuant to Section 83(b) of the Internal Revenue Code of 1986, as amended (the "Code") and pursuant to the corresponding provisions, if any, of applicable state law; or

(b) ___has knowingly chosen not to consult such a tax advisor.

3.   The undersigned hereby states that the undersigned has decided [check as applicable]:

(a) ___ to make an election pursuant to Section 83(b) of the Code, and is submitting to the Company, together with the undersigned's executed Restricted Stock Purchase Agreement, an executed form entitled "Election Under Section 83(b) of the Internal Revenue Code of 1986;" or

(b) ___ not to make an election pursuant to Section 83(b) of the Code.

4.   Neither the Company nor any subsidiary or representative of the Company has made any warranty or representation to the undersigned with respect to the tax consequences of the undersigned's purchase of the Shares or of the making or failure to make an election pursuant to Section 83(b) of the Code or the corresponding provisions, if any, of applicable state law.

Dated:_____   PURCHASER:

Name:_____

_____
(Signature)

Address:

_____
_____

Email: _____

_____
Spouse of Purchaser (if applicable)

EXHIBIT C

ELECTION UNDER SECTION 83(b)
OF THE INTERNAL REVENUE CODE OF 1986

Instructions: *If Purchaser is making the 83(b) election, he or she may do by filling out and sending this form to the IRS within 30 days of the transfer.*

The undersigned taxpayer hereby elects, pursuant to Section 83(b) of the Internal Revenue Code, to include in taxpayer's gross income or alternative minimum taxable income, as applicable, for the current taxable year, the amount of any income that may be taxable to taxpayer in connection with taxpayer's receipt of the property described below:

1.   The name, address, taxpayer identification number and taxable year of the undersigned are as follows:

NAME OF TAXPAYER: _____

NAME   OF   SPOUSE: _____

ADDRESS: _____

IDENTIFICATION NO. OF TAXPAYER: _____

IDENTIFICATION NO. OF SPOUSE: _____

TAXABLE YEAR: _____

2.   The property with respect to which the election is made is described as follows:

_____ shares of Class _____ stock of _____, Inc., a Delaware corporation (the "Company").

3.   The date on which the property was transferred is: _____

4.   The property is subject to the following restrictions:

Repurchase option at cost in favor of the Company upon termination of taxpayer's employment or consulting relationship.

5.   The fair market value at the time of transfer, determined without regard to any restriction other than a restriction which by its terms will never lapse, of such property is: _____

33

6.   The amount (if any) paid for such property: _____ (in cash, services previously rendered or a combination) [Note to the reader: if the value of such property equals value of services rendered, there are tax benefits for both parties)

The undersigned has submitted a copy of this statement to the person for whom the services were performed in connection with the undersigned's receipt of the above-described property.   The transferee of such property is the person performing the services in connection with the transfer of said property.

The undersigned understands that the foregoing election may not be revoked except with the consent of the Commissioner.

Dated:_____   Purchaser:

                                 Name:_____

                                 (Signature)

                                 Address:

                                 _____
                                 _____

                                 Email: _____

                                 _____
                                 Spouse of Purchaser (if applicable)

RECEIPT

Instructions: *Please provide this and the stock certificate to Purchaser upon receipt of the payment for the shares.*

_____ Inc., a Delaware corporation (the "Company"), hereby acknowledges receipt of _____ (in cash, services previously rendered, or a combination of the foregoing) as consideration for Certificate No. CS ____ for _____ Class ____ shares of stock of the Company.

Dated:_____   THE COMPANY:

                                      _____ INC.

                                      By:_____
                                                (Signature)

                                      Name:_____
                                      Title:_____

RECEIPT AND CONSENT

Instructions: *Please have Purchaser fill this out and return to the Company upon receipt of the shares.*

The undersigned hereby acknowledges receipt of a photocopy of Certificate No. CS _____ for _____Class B shares of stock _____, Inc., a Delaware corporation (the "Company"). These shares represent _____% of the fully diluted outstanding shares

The undersigned further acknowledges that the Secretary of the Company, or his

or her designee, is acting as escrow holder pursuant to the Restricted Stock Purchase

Agreement that Purchaser has previously entered into with the Company. As escrow

holder, the Secretary of the Company, or his or her designee, holds the original of the

aforementioned certificate issued in the undersigned's name.

Dated:_____   PURCHASER:

Name:_____

_____
(Signature)

Email:_____

_____
Spouse of Purchaser (if applicable)

-----------End of Exhibit 1: Stock purchase agreement--------

----- **Exhibit 2: Separation Terms** -----

_____, INC

2016 SEPARATION TERM SHEET

This is supposed to be an open opportunity to get in. But we understand sometimes, we are called to part ways.

As it is agreed upon through all documents, the contractual relationship can be terminated at any time by both The Contractor and The Company.

The separation terms outlined below shall be the final terms of separation in regards to the relationship with the Company.

All intellectual property and work performed belongs to the Company with no claims of any revenues.

If separation happens prior to any shares Vesting: Contractor leaves with nothing. All unvested shares are forfeited for $_____ to the Company.

If separation occurs AFTER vesting of any shares (After the 1st year Anniversary of the vesting Schedule)

- Contractor keeps the shares and payment terms remain as agreed on vested shares.
- All unvested shares will be forfeited and reacquired by the company for a flat $_____ as a good faith of separation.
- Respect of the Non-Disclosure relationship and all good faith relationship in case of separation with the Company.

------End of Exhibit 2: Separation Agreement –

----- Exhibit 3: Additional and Final disclosures -----

The opportunity to participate in our very exciting project probably comes with some questions at this stage to fully understand what the documents you have been sent represent. For the sake of full transparency and for the ability

Please find below several material facts about _____, Inc. ("The Company). Please maintain this information within the limits of the Non-Disclosure agreement you have signed. Some of this information is deemed company private property and should only be discussed (if needed) with your counsel solely in the view of making a final decision on joining The _____ project.

The Company _____, Inc. is a Delaware Corporation, incorporated in _____(year) whose mailing address is _____. We are a _____(company description).

The Company has a total_____Authorized shares.

DETAIL OF STOCK CLASSES AND WEIGHTS OPTIONAL, BUT WE RECOMMEND AND ENCOURAGE A FULLY TRANSPARENT DISCLOSURE

The par Value of the shares is $_____ / share

The high number of shares is intrinsically related to the long term vision of the company to open its stock ownership to a large number of individuals over a period of time.

Current Outstanding shares as of this offering are: _____ **outstanding Shares including Class C, Class A, and Class B types of Stock.**

Part of the strategy of the company is not to AUTHORIZE any more shares for the life of the Company. In the unlikely event that such an event, or split, or any event that will affect the weight of shares, the company guarantees it will maintain the weight of each individual shareholder proportionate to what it was prior to the unlikely event.

The founder, CEO, Director and sole officer of the Company is _____ who holds 52% of the total authorized shares by the company, retaining full control on the company in view of aggressive market penetration and consolidation of all decision making in one person and to ensure company integrity as we evolve.

_____ Info about Founder

Info about any co-founder / associates holding more than 5% of the stock.

Main Shareholders and strategy of share allocations (optional but recommended for transaparency)

_____ of founder/ inventor:_____

_____ reserved for talent attraction (contractors) and Employee incentive plans in the future.

_____ left for future developments, funds attraction, or to be distributed by the Company as it sees fit based on the evolution.

Company's business plan is to _____

The Company also aims at _____

Our business plan aims to _____

This and all documents once reviewed and accepted by you, will be officially drafted and official sealed copies will be made available for you to sign and enter in contract with The Company.

As we will engage in doing business, please bear in mind the following risks prior to committing to this project.

A. Risks Relating to the Financial Condition of the Company.

1. The Company has no expectation for immediate profits.

2. The Company has generated limited operating revenues.

3. The Company is minimally capitalized.

4. A substantial portion of the Company's assets are comprised of intangible items.

5. The Company is dependent on the generations of revenues and or fundraising to continue operations in the long term.

6. The Company faces adverse consequences if generation of revenues and/or fundraising are not successful.

B. Risks Relating to the Business of the Company.

1. The Company is a start-up company in the development stage: The company is in a start-up period (developmental stage) and has not engaged in any significant operations to date. There is no certainty that the company will be successful in overcoming the substantial risks as set forth below in order to advance beyond the start-up period (developmental stage).

2. It is uncertain whether a market exists or will develop for the Company's product or service.

3. The Company's product and business are unproven.

4. The Company faces competition from existing entities in similar business which have greater resources.

5. The Company has limited or no manufacturing capability.

6. The Company's products or services are subject to governmental regulation (e.g. licensing, environmental, etc.).

7. The Company faces risks relating to technological obsolescence.

8. The Company may need to rely on revenue generation and/or outside financing.

11. The Company is dependent on the efforts of management.

C. Risks Relating to Management of the Company

1. Principal of the Company has no prior records in similar business.

2. Absolute voting control of the Company will be retained by founder, keeping a 52% stake in the overall authorized share pool.

D. Risks Relating to the Securities being Offered and the Terms of the Offering.

- You face the risk of loss of your entire shares.
- The Company's securities are not publicly traded and there can be no assurance that a market will develop.

---- End of Exhibit 3: Additional Disclosures -----

As a concluding note: Please note all this information is meant only to provide an overall introduction and general canvas for our proposed communitarian model.

No material in this book is aimed at replacing legal advice from an attorney, or fiscal advice from a tax advisor. We aim at sharing the entrepreneurial journey we undertook, no more, no less.

May every dreamer get to live the entrepreneurial journey of building his dream.

Freely.

Remain Innocent – Make New Ways

Sunnyvale, Nov 2nd 2016